A KID'S LIFE DURING

THE WESTWARD EXPANSION

SARAH MACHAJEWSKI

PowerKiDS press.

New York

Published in 2015 by The Rosen Publishing Group, Inc.
29 East 21st Street, New York, NY 10010

First Edition

Editor: Sarah Machajewski
Book Design: Michael J. Flynn

Photo Credits: Cover De Agostini Picture Library/Getty Images; cover, pp. 1, 3, 4, 6–10, 12, 14, 16–18, 20, 22–24 (background texture) Ozerina Anna/Shutterstock.com; pp. 3, 4, 6–10, 12, 14, 16–18, 20, 22–24 (paper) Paladin12/Shutterstock.com; p. 5 FPG/Archive Photos/Getty Images; p. 6 MPI/Archive Photos/Getty Images; pp. 7, 9 courtesy of the Library of Congress; p. 10 Joe Gough/Shutterstock.com; p. 11 Michael Shake/Shutterstock.com; p. 13 Tim Abramowitz/E+/Getty Images; p. 15 © North Wind Picture Archives; p. 16 © iStockphoto/bradwieland; p. 17 Chiyacat/Shutterstock.com; p. 19 Ron Blanton/Shutterstock.com; p. 21 The Bridgeman Art Library/Getty Images; p. 22 Zack Frank/Shutterstock.com.

Library of Congress Cataloging-in-Publication Data

Machajewski, Sarah.
A kid's life during the Westward Expansion / by Sarah Machajewski.
p. cm. — (How kids lived)
Includes index.
ISBN 978-1-4994-0022-9 (pbk.)
ISBN 978-1-4994-0011-3 (6-pack)
ISBN 978-1-4994-0013-7 (library binding)
1. Children — United States — Social life and customs — 19th century — Juvenile literature 2. West (U.S.) — Social life and customs — Juvenile literature. 3. Frontier and pioneer life — West (U.S.) — Juvenile literature. I. Machajewski, Sarah. II. Title.
F596.M34 2015
977.02—d23

Manufactured in the United States of America

CPSIA Compliance Information: Batch #CW15PK: For Further Information contact Rosen Publishing, New York, New York at 1-800-237-9932

CONTENTS

GOING WEST

The United States became an independent nation in 1783. The population quickly outgrew the land that made up the original country. Some Americans took it upon themselves to tame unsettled land west of the Mississippi River. These **pioneers** settled the western **frontier** during a period that's now known as the westward **expansion**.

Pioneers packed their lives into wagons. They brought the tools they needed to survive and belongings they didn't want to leave behind. They didn't know what they would find, but left in hopes of finding new opportunities out west.

Many families, including children and babies, went west in order to start a new life.

TRAVEL BY WAGON

Westward expansion began in the mid-1800s. Hundreds of thousands of people left the eastern United States and set out for Oregon, California, and other territories in between. Groups of pioneers traveled in covered wagon trains, which sometimes included 30 wagons!

Teams of oxen pulled covered wagons. They were strong enough to pull heavy loads.

The journey west was hard. There were no roads. Traveling depended on the weather, and the wagon trains moved slowly. On a good, clear day, pioneers traveled no more than 20 miles (32 km). Many children made the trip west with their families. They often walked alongside the wagons.

THE WILD FRONTIER

Paul was a pioneer kid. He made the journey west with his mom, dad, and sister. Paul's family came from Missouri. They packed all their belongings into a covered wagon. After many months, his family finally reached the area that's now Montana.

There were many **resources** for Paul's family to use. However, they were very hard to gather at first. Like other pioneers, Paul's family hunted and gathered wild fruit and nuts until they could grow their own food. Paul helped his dad clear the land of trees. They used this land to plant crops and build a home.

Growing food was more important than building houses. Pioneers camped out until the plowing and planting were done.

BIG FAMILIES

Pioneer families were usually very large. Lots of children meant there were lots of people to help out!

BUILDING A HOME

The pioneers didn't waste anything. They used the trees cleared from the forests to build log cabins. Everyone in the wagon train helped build the houses. Men cut the logs in a special way so they fit together. The roof, floor, and door were all made of wood, too. Paul and his sister Mary filled the gaps between the logs with clay, mud, and moss. This kept the cabin warm and dry.

Pioneers also built barns out of wood. The barns housed animals, such as horses, oxen, cows, and sheep.

Stacking logs this way made pioneer homes strong and sturdy.

Log cabins and barns were built to be strong. They kept people and animals safe from cold, heat, rain, and other kinds of weather.

LIFE IN A LOG CABIN

The inside of a log cabin was very simple. Every cabin had a fireplace with a stone **hearth**. Pioneers used the fireplace to heat the cabin and cook food. Paul's dad made a table and chairs that were kept near the fireplace.

Paul and Mary slept in a **loft** above the kitchen. They used a ladder to climb up and down from it. They shared a bed that was made of **canvas** filled with dried leaves. The bed rested on two thick logs, which kept it off the floor. They hung their clothes on wooden pegs along the wall.

MAKING ROOM

Brothers and sisters often shared a bed, since there wasn't enough space for everyone to have their own.

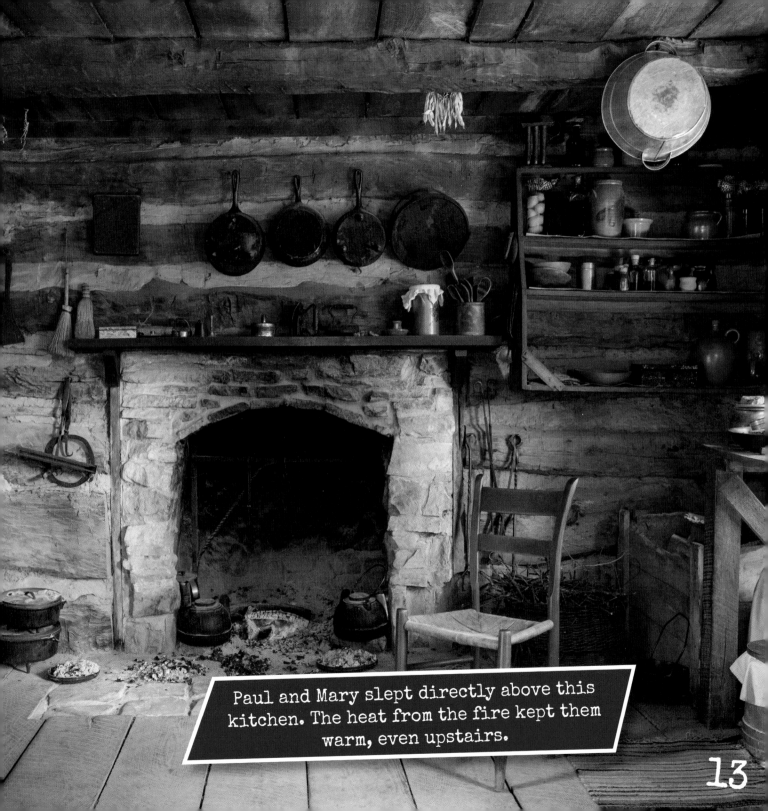

Paul and Mary slept directly above this kitchen. The heat from the fire kept them warm, even upstairs.

PIONEER CHORES

Being a kid in pioneer times was a lot of work. Paul and Mary had chores every day. Paul fed the farm animals and brought in wood for the fire—all before breakfast! Mary gathered eggs from the chicken coop. She and her mother used them to make breakfast. They made corn cakes, too.

Paul and Mary got back to work right after breakfast. Paul helped his father in the fields and cared for the animals. Mary milked the cows. She used the milk to make butter. Mary and her mom also made clothes from different kinds of cloth.

HARD AT WORK

Pioneer children were put to work as soon as they were old enough to help, usually by the time they were four or five years old.

The work never ended on the western frontier. Kids had chores every day, even on the weekends and holidays!

ALL ABOUT CLOTHING

Pioneers dressed in clothes that made sense for their surroundings and the weather. In general, women and girls wore dresses, **petticoats**, and aprons. They wore big **bonnets** to guard their faces and necks from the sun. They wore **shawls** in winter.

Pioneer girls and boys dressed like their parents.

Pioneers had to know how to use everything in their surroundings, including animals.

Men and boys wore pants and long shirts made of whatever cloth the women made. The sun was strong and hot during the day, so they wore straw hats when they worked in the fields. Paul had a hat made of raccoon fur. He caught the raccoon and used its fur to make a hat.

SCHOOLS IN THE WEST

School wasn't very important in the earliest days of westward expansion. That's because there weren't enough people to make up a small town! Parents taught their children the skills they needed to survive.

Like most pioneer boys, Paul learned how to use an ax and a **rifle**. He also learned how to make and fix tools. Like most pioneer girls, Mary learned how to cook, sew, and make cloth. Children learned the alphabet and numbers from the Bible. Schools were built once enough families had settled in one area. They were often one-room schoolhouses.

Most teachers in the West had moved there from the East to teach.

PIONEER SCHOOLS

Students of all ages were in the same classroom together. The youngest kids sat up front, and the oldest sat in back. Boys and girls sat on opposite sides of the room.

MIXING WORK AND PLAY

Life on the western frontier was so busy that sometimes it felt like there wasn't time for fun, but pioneers found ways to mix work and play. Families gathered together for barn-raising parties. They celebrated with food, music, and dancing when the barn was finished.

Pioneer women and girls often had **quilting bees**. Each woman made a piece of the quilt. When all the pieces were put together, it made a beautiful quilt. The quilts were often given as gifts to people in their community.

Music was a big part of pioneer gatherings. Paul's dad played the fiddle, another name for a violin, at these events.

TIME FOR FUN

Pioneer kids often made their own toys. They also played outside, doing fun things like swimming or playing games in the fields.

A NEW PATH

Life during westward expansion wasn't easy. Families had to depend on each other in order to survive. If a pioneer family needed food, medicine, or help with building their home, other pioneer families were there to help.

As time went on, life on the western frontier became a little easier. More people settled, and small communities grew into towns. Soon, there were more people to help tame the West. But the original pioneers, like Paul and Mary's family, helped create paths that many other Americans followed.

GLOSSARY

bonnet: A woman's or girl's cloth hat that ties under the chin, usually with strings or ribbons.

canvas: A strong cloth.

expansion: The act of becoming larger.

frontier: The wilderness that lies beyond the edge of settled territory.

hearth: The area in front of a fireplace.

loft: An upper room or space open to the area below.

petticoat: A slip worn under a skirt or dress.

pioneer: A person who is among the first to explore or settle a new area.

quilting bee: A fun event in which women gathered to create quilts.

resource: Something in nature that can be used by people.

rifle: A long gun that is fired from the shoulder.

shawl: A piece of women's clothing that's worn around the shoulders or head.

INDEX

WEBSITES

Due to the changing nature of Internet links, PowerKids Press has developed an online list of websites related to the subject of this book. This site is updated regularly. Please use this link to access the list: www.powerkidslinks.com/hkl/west